My Kitten Only Poops at Midnight

And Other Tails from SOS Cat Rescue AZ

Written by Bianca Maubach
Founder, SOS Cat Rescue AZ

**My Kitten Only Poops at Midnight
And Other Tails from SOS Cat Rescue AZ**

Author: Bianca Maubach
Contributors: Todd Cohen and Samuel Molina
Published by SOS Cat Rescue AZ, Inc.

Copyright © 2020 SOS Cat Rescue AZ, Inc. All rights reserved. No portion of this book may be reproduced in any form without permission from the publisher, except as permitted by U.S. copyright law.

For permission contact:

SOS Cat Rescue AZ, Inc.
P.O. Box 35002
Tucson, AZ 85740-5002

Info@SOSCatRescueAZ.org
www.SOSCatRescueAZ.org

ISBN-13: 978-0-578-61893-7

Dedication

This book is dedicated to the kittens and cats who have been rescued and all the ones who are still out there needing our help.

SOS Cat Rescue AZ, Inc. is a foster-based, volunteer-run 501(c)(3) non-profit animal rescue group based out of Tucson, AZ dedicated to Saving Orphan kittens and Senior cats from shelters across Arizona and giving them a second chance for a "happily ever after" life by matching adoptable kitties to the right homes. All cats are solely placed in foster homes where they will be taken care of according to their individual needs such as bottle feeding for orphans, socialization for kittens while growing up, medical attention to the sick, and hospice care for seniors.

All proceeds from this book will be donated to SOS Cat Rescue AZ to help care for the extremely lucky kitties who arrive at their doorstep.

The stories contained herein are true stories from SOS Cat Rescue AZ foster homes. Names have been removed to protect the guilty "pawties". Please follow their latest escapades on social media and our website!

https://SOSCatRescueAZ.org

 @SOSCatRescueAZ

Donations gladly accepted at www.paypal.me/4SOS

My cat figured out that if my purse is on the kitchen counter, I will soon leave the house for hours, perhaps never to return. One day, after I cut snuggles short and placed my purse on the counter to grab my to-go coffee cup, he jumped up and peed in my purse! Now my purse hangs on a special hook to prevent another episode. This has not stopped him from trying.

My cat requires her litter box to be filled with lots of litter since she will dig for a long time to make a nice hole. She doesn't like shallow holes and her digs must be perfect excavations. She will dig for up to 15 min before she is satisfied with the shape and size before she empties her bladder.

My kitten prefers her canned food heated on the stove instead of in the microwave. Offering her microwaved food may result in a hunger strike. Offering cold food will result in death (of the human).

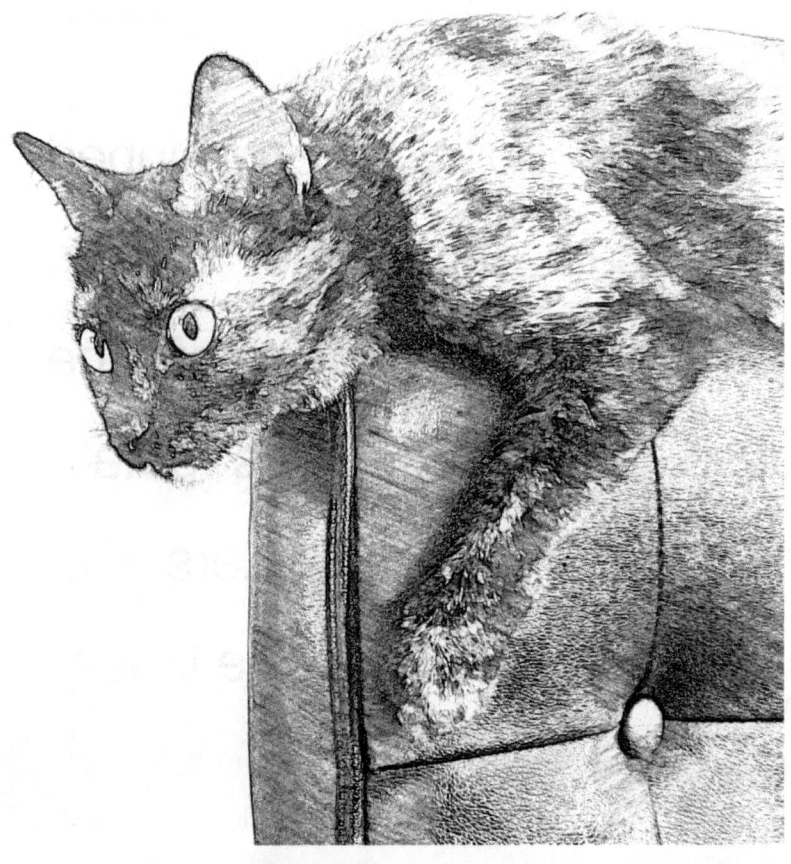

My kitten heard the whipped cream can and came running from the other side of the house. She also loves potato chips and cheese crackers. Cat food is only for desperate times.

My kitten polished off a whole can of kitten food then went to take a nap on the bed. Ten minutes later when I opened a can for his sister, he came running. He was starving.

My kitty is high maintenance. She needs two litter boxes (at a minimum) because she goes #1 in one and #2 in the other. All hell breaks loose if she needs to go #1 again and the box is not cleaned. She will relieve herself in front of the box. I have catered to her needs by adding two more boxes.

My cat is picky about the brand and the location of her food. After I've purchased the approved brand of wet food, she will not tolerate it being near the dry food, nor even in the kitchen! If the wet food bowl is near the dry food bowl, she will turn her nose up and walk away. Only when her wet food is moved into a completely different room will she express her appreciation by eating it as quickly as possible.

My kitten left a small, white present in the litter box. I couldn't remember when I fed her rice. Then, it dawned on me. It wasn't rice! (Hint: giardia)

My kitten was sick and lethargic for days. When I took her to the vet she started purring, jumping around, and acting like a healthy kitten. Now my vet knows I'm crazy.

My senior foster cat is convinced that she doesn't need medication, despite the explosive diarrhea she experiences with every sneeze. She performs alligator rolls while wrapped up in a blanket just to avoid her medicine. Our sweet, 7-pound kitty squared off with the two vet techs during her last appointment and nearly won.

My kitten likes my friends more than me. She must have read my text to a friend that we were coming over to visit because she suddenly jumped up and ran into her carrier.

My kitten argues for real food when I lazily give her treats first thing in the morning. She's very judgmental when I don't provide proper nutrition, or exactly what she wants when she wants it.

My new home seemed a little empty, so I brought home a little black kitten with a crooked tail. She immediately became besties with my black lab. A few days later when I couldn't find her anywhere, I finally implored my pup to help look for her. He looked up and from beneath his long fur another little head with bright yellow eyes popped up and looked at me. Now I always know where she can be found.

My kitten prefers to dine on Wedgwood crystal but will settle for fine china.

My kitten can't possibly sleep unless she's snuggling on my neck. The boogie monsters are real. So is her drool.

My cat had been living outside for several years before she adopted our home. After living inside for three days she began running under the bed anytime someone approached a door. She is NOT going back outside ever again.

My kitten was fiercely attacking the blankets until she suddenly fell asleep, tooth still snagged on the blanket, and visions of saving the world in her dreams.

My kitten was very sick and had diarrhea. The vet asked me to bring in a stool sample within four hours of "delivery". Since I was off work for the next three days, this should have been easy. That's when my kitten decided that she only poops at midnight.
#MyKittenOnlyPoopsAtMidnight

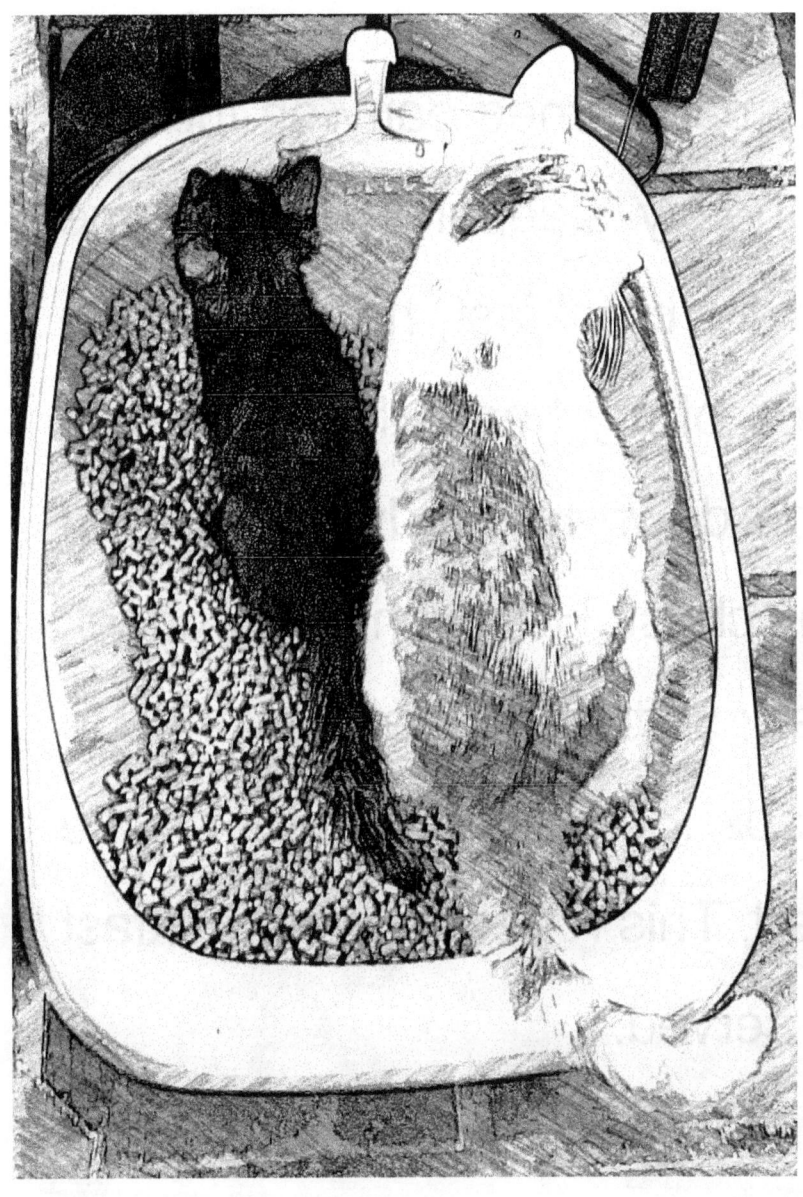

My cat learned early on that I'm a heavy sleeper. To wake me up for breakfast, he lays on the side of my head, then walks up and down my body and sits on my chest. He touches my cheek very softly and then, wham! He slaps me hard and runs off the bed. This repeats until breakfast is served.

My 20-ounce chronically ill kitten won't eat the same food two days in a row. We must keep three different kinds of food available to prevent a hunger strike which would jeopardize her health.

My Kitten Only Poops at Midnight

My cat inspects my bath very carefully. He can't understand why I would fill this big box with water, and then get into it.

My kitten loves food so much that every day from age 6 - 8 weeks he fell asleep with his face in his canned food. He vehemently protested my cleaning the dried food out of his whiskers after the nap. He was trying to save it for later. You never know when the food source will suddenly dry up.

My kitten needs one pill twice per day. She hides the pill in her cheek and pretends to swallow to fool me. She waits a few seconds, or minutes, and then trots away to spit the pill out on the floor in plain sight.

My newest foster kitten is a tiny replica of our flame point Siamese. Baby Buddy follows Big Buddy around mimicking his every move, even tail movements.

My cat thinks I'm a terrible provider. She proved it by catching a fish from my neighbor's koi pond and carrying it up a spiral staircase, across my downstairs neighbor's balcony, up a 2x4 plank set at an angle to the third story, and right inside my house. That wasn't all she brought!

My Kitten Only Poops at Midnight | 57

My cats enjoyed chewing on the humidifier wires until I bought a motion-sensing air puffer. My girl learned after one puff, but my boy was a little slower. He repeatedly got puffed by air and screamed at the offending puff, demanding that I remove the enemy.

My Kitten Only Poops at Midnight

My foster kitten had a visitor one day. He immediately lunged at her and started purring. We knew immediately that he had chosen his new mom.

My kitten recently started copycatting my burger-stealing dogs. I turned away from my plate for a moment, and when I returned, the bun was askew, and the patty was gone. Looking around for a dog to blame, I spied my kitten halfway down the hall, chomping on the edge of the patty. When she saw me, she tried to run away again, tripping and hobbling over the patty still firmly in her mouth.

My Kitten Only Poops at Midnight

My resident Tortie doesn't mind most foster kittens, but she took offense to one particular Tortie kitten. They often stared at each other for hours, neither one willing to give in.
#NeverTooManyTorties

My kitten sits quietly in my lap all day while I'm working in my home office. I talk to various people throughout the day and not a peep from him. As soon as I get a call from my boss, the kitten raises his voice to be heard too. Once my boss asked if a baby was crying.

My Kitten Only Poops at Midnight

My sweet kitty was constipated for quite a while. Nothing seemed to help. One night she hopped up on my chest and I started scratching her head. She purred so loudly, so I scratched harder. She was really into it! Apparently, the excitement loosened her up because everything came out right on my chest!

My kitten needs nasal drops twice per day. She hates it so much. When I get the bottle out, we emit simultaneous sighs.

My cat was feral before deciding to adopt us. Somewhere she picked up an obsession for Krispy Kreme birthday cake donuts. While she will eat any donut left unattended, she can smell the Krispy Kreme birthday cake donut as soon as it enters the house and will actually steal it out of my mouth!

My kitten prefers brand name tissues when she has a stuffy nose. Only the softest will do. Naturally.

My Kitten Only Poops at Midnight

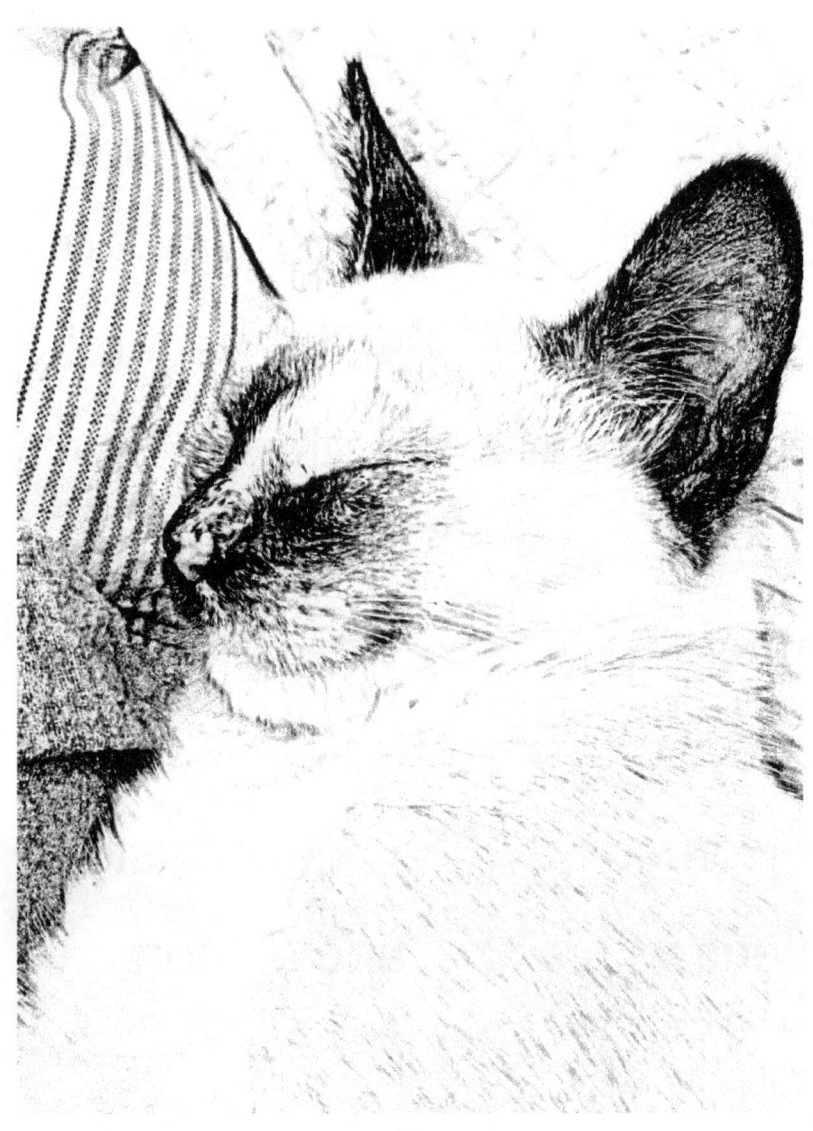

My cat was rescued from his birth home which housed 40 cats! When I visited the general population room at the shelter 15 years ago, he spotted me immediately and attacked any cat who came near me. Now he welcomes all the new foster kittens with a sniff and a snort.

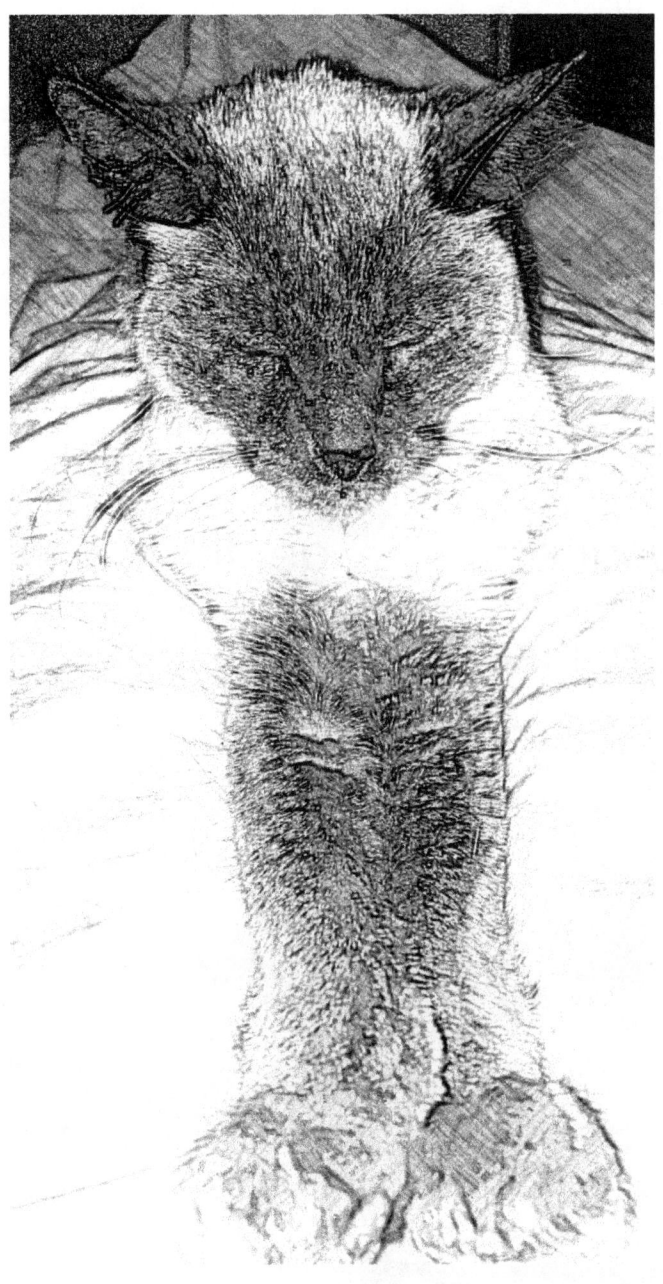

My cat only snuggles with Rubenesque gentlemen. Everyone else is obviously out to get her.

My kitty is nocturnal. At night, she plays with her toys, eats, and wanders around the house opening drawers and closet doors. Occasionally, she wants company and stands at the foot of the bed meowing. When I pat the bed, she jumps up on my chest, purring loudly until I am fully awake. After 5 minutes she is off to play again leaving me wide awake. That is, until she notices that I'm asleep again.

My Tortie sisters love to take a shower with me. Once when I finished before they could join in, they cried and cried until I turned the shower on again. They would not calm down until I got back in the shower with them. #NeverTooManyTorties

My cat became attached to me very quickly and now wants to go with me everywhere.

My foster kitties love their new house with floor-to-ceiling windows. They chirp at every fowl or beast that comes near, warning of their legendary hunting skills.

My foster kitten yells at me during feeding time or anytime I walk by a food bowl. I must throw at least ten dry food kernels, one at a time, for her to chase down and eat. This goes only one of two ways: she either eats them all and moves on or she will follow me around screaming at me.

When I walk towards a certain part of our house my kitten chases me down to play fetch. To show that she means business she brings her toy mice and drops them in front of me. Let's hope she sticks with the toys.

My Kitten Only Poops at Midnight

One of my foster kittens sits at dinner with us gently putting her paw towards the plate and/or touching the hand with the fork to let me know she wants my food. She knows she is not allowed on the table, so she sits patiently in the chair next to me. She knows that she is adorable and completely irresistible.

One of my kittens patiently waits for us to finish dinner and he then pre-cleans the dishes prior to going in the dishwasher. He's doing one heck of a job.

It's a good thing we purchased a 360 water fountain only to have a kitty want to drink out of our sinks only. For her, only the freshest water is acceptable.

One of our foster cats ate his meal so quickly (because he thought he wouldn't get enough) that he'd throw-up instantly. Once we put the food on separate plates, he slowed down and all was good. Some cats just don't want to share plates.

My vet wanted a sample of my hospice cat's explosive diarrhea. I followed behind her with the collection cup until she 'let loose'. After several days of unsuccessful 'events', I finally caught enough stool to satisfy the vet. Be careful what you wish for.

Kiki's Story

The title was inspired by a frustrating experience with a severely ill, 3-week-old, orphaned bottle baby kitten who struggled to thrive for months and who just would not cooperate with her vet, Dr. Shear, when he needed a fresh sample for testing. After nearly a year of poor health and many scares since she was just such a fragile kitten, the staff at Twin Peaks Veterinary Center, our rescue veterinary center, were successful in saving Kiki's life and stabilizing her health. They affectionately dubbed her "Spitfire" because of her tenacious spirit.

Now, after 2 years, Ms. Keeks (her preferred nickname as noted by loud purrs and affection) is finally thriving in her now permanent residence with her foster mom and welcomes new litters of orphaned kittens into the SOS family. Ms. Keeks is living her best life and only goes on a hunger strike when she misses her favorite vet, Dr. Shear. Thank you for the outstanding service and veterinary care for all SOS kitties!

We hope you have enjoyed our tails today!
Share your stories on Facebook.
#MyKittenOnlyPoopsAtMidnight

https://SOSCatRescueAZ.org

 @SOSCatRescueAZ

Donations gladly accepted at
www.paypal.me/4SOS

SOS Cat Rescue AZ
P.O. Box 35002
Tucson, AZ 85740-5002

www.ingramcontent.com/pod-product-compliance
Lightning Source LLC
Chambersburg PA
CBHW070513090426
42735CB00012B/2768